I0144092

www.thegreatchiweenie.com

The Great chiweenie Presents: Coasting Along. Copyright © 2009 by Gu and Cubby Cashen. All Rights Reserved. No part of this book including photographs may be reprinted, reproduced or transmitted in any form or by any electronic means without written permission from the publisher. Brief quotations used in critical articles or reviews are permissible. For more information, please contact , The Great Chiweenie Productions, P.O. Box 669, Cambria, California 93428. www.thegreatchiweenie.com.

ISBN-13 978-0-9814900-2-1
ISBN-10 0-9814900-2-6

All Photographs by: Casey Cordes, Cubby Cashen and Megan Cordes.

WARNING: Riding a bicycle can be dangerous. Please wear all safety equipment and follow all the laws and regulations when riding a bicycle. Gu is safely harnessed into the backpack in which he rides, but is still at risk of injury due to any accidents or falls. Wear a helmet. PLEASE RIDE SAFE.

Teachers, Principals, and Businesses, for bulk purchasing or promotionals, please contact Cubby at thegreatchiweenie@hotmail.com.

The Great Chiweenie presents

COASTING ALONG

by GU and Clubby Cashen

The Great Chiweenie Productions
P.O. Box 669
Cambria, CA 93428
thegreatchiweenie@hotmail.com
www.thegreatchiweenie.com

Note from the Author:

Hey! My Name is Gu, a.k.a. "The Great Chiweenie" (Act like the I is silent CH-Weenie). I am part-dachshund and part-chihuahua and I travel with my adopted parents, Megan and Cub. This is my second picture book, but this time we had help from Megan's little brother, Casey. He joined our pack and drove our stuff, took pictures, and helped when needed. Megan helped me put my words together more this time while I really don't know what Cub had to do with this. We enjoyed meeting all our new friends as we rode from San Francisco to our hometown, Cambria. Hope you enjoy!

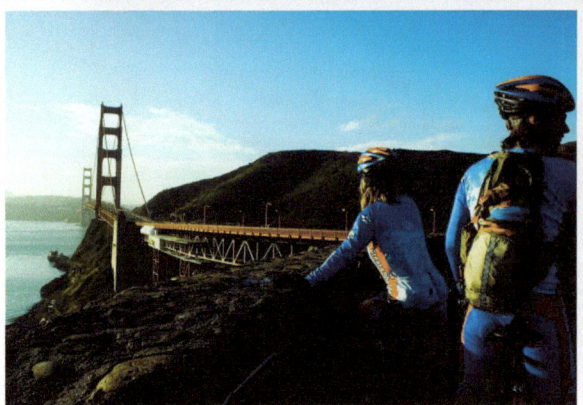

We start in San Francisco
a place everybody knows.
Its got a giant bridge
and smells like sourdough.

1

Day 1, is sure my favorite.
We are full of energy.
Excited for the things to come,
the smells and things we see.

We head towards the ocean
and hardly feel a breeze.
Cold, clear and beautiful
as far as our eyes can see.

Meg makes me wear a sweater
in order to keep warm.
It always does the trick though,
even in a storm.

But there's no storm ahead
as we proceed to ride
into what seems wilderness
with wide and open skies.

5

But trouble comes our way
a few miles apart.
Our flat tires must be fixed
before we could restart.

Finally, its time to stop
as the evening closes in.
Its time to rest our tired paws,
with hopes of sleeping in.

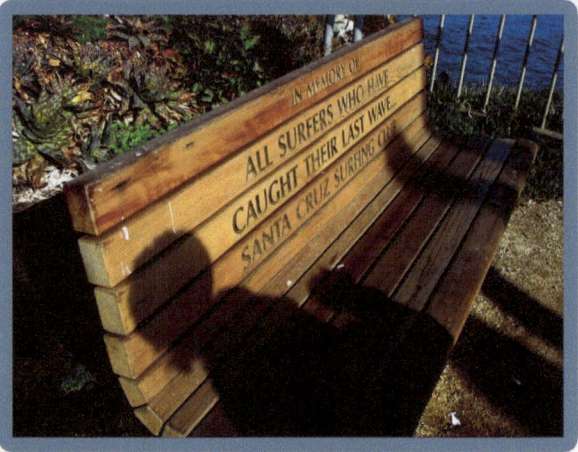

We sleep until the sun wakes us
in the land of banana slugs.
We fill ourselves with breakfast,
and drink water by the jug.

Its back on the bikes
as we head around the bay.
Today is all about the farms
and things we see on the way.

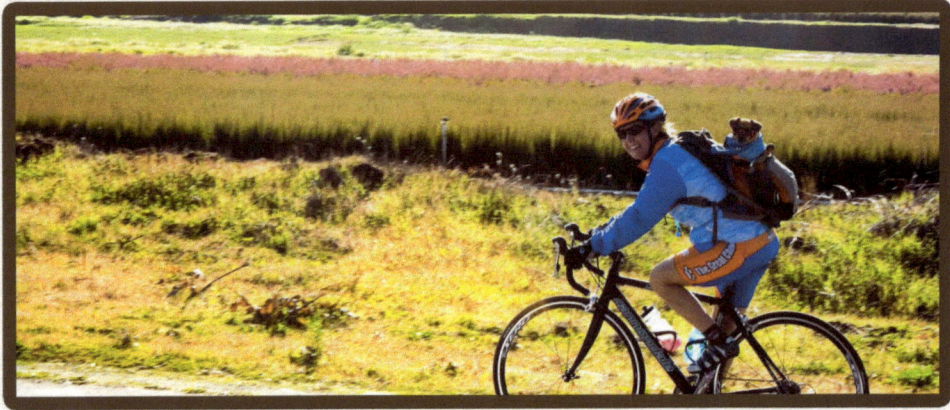

Their bums are really sore today
Cub and Megan agree.
They stand up on their pedals,
creating achy knees.

We try to guess the foods
that were planted by the row.
Broccoli, lettuce, cauliflower,
artichoke and avocado?

The comforts of the bike path,
replace the busy street.
We weave between the sand dunes
where the land and ocean meet.

El Chiweenie

18

Megan and Cub are tired,
but not as much as me.
As we pull into our campground,
I leave the pack, I'm free!

We start by setting up the tent
as the sun goes down.
In go the sleeping bags,
I'm in bed without a sound.

The epic stretch of Big Sur coast,
was about to come.
Rugged cliffs and unreal views,
our hearts beat like a drum.

People come from here and there,
they stop to take a pic.
Cameras out and ready to roll,
like I was 'bout to do a trick.

NEXT 74 MILES

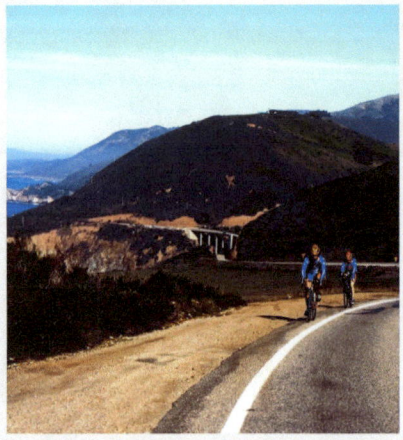

Crossing bridges and going slow
as we climb the hills,
topping off around the corners,
downhills lead to thrills.

19

One more night to sleep
outside near the sea.
Cold, chilly and crystal clear,
in the den I would be.

The warmest day of the trip,
would get us to the end.
Passing lighthouses and seals,
the wind would be our friend.

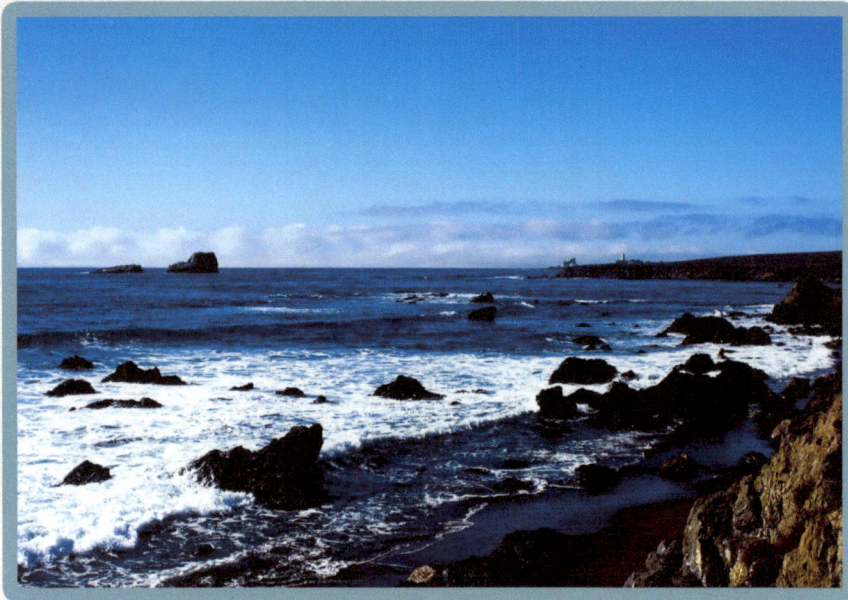

Sniff, it smells like Cambria.
I think we're getting close.
The buildings look familiar now,
I think we're there, almost.

Cambria
POP 6,444   ELEV 60

28

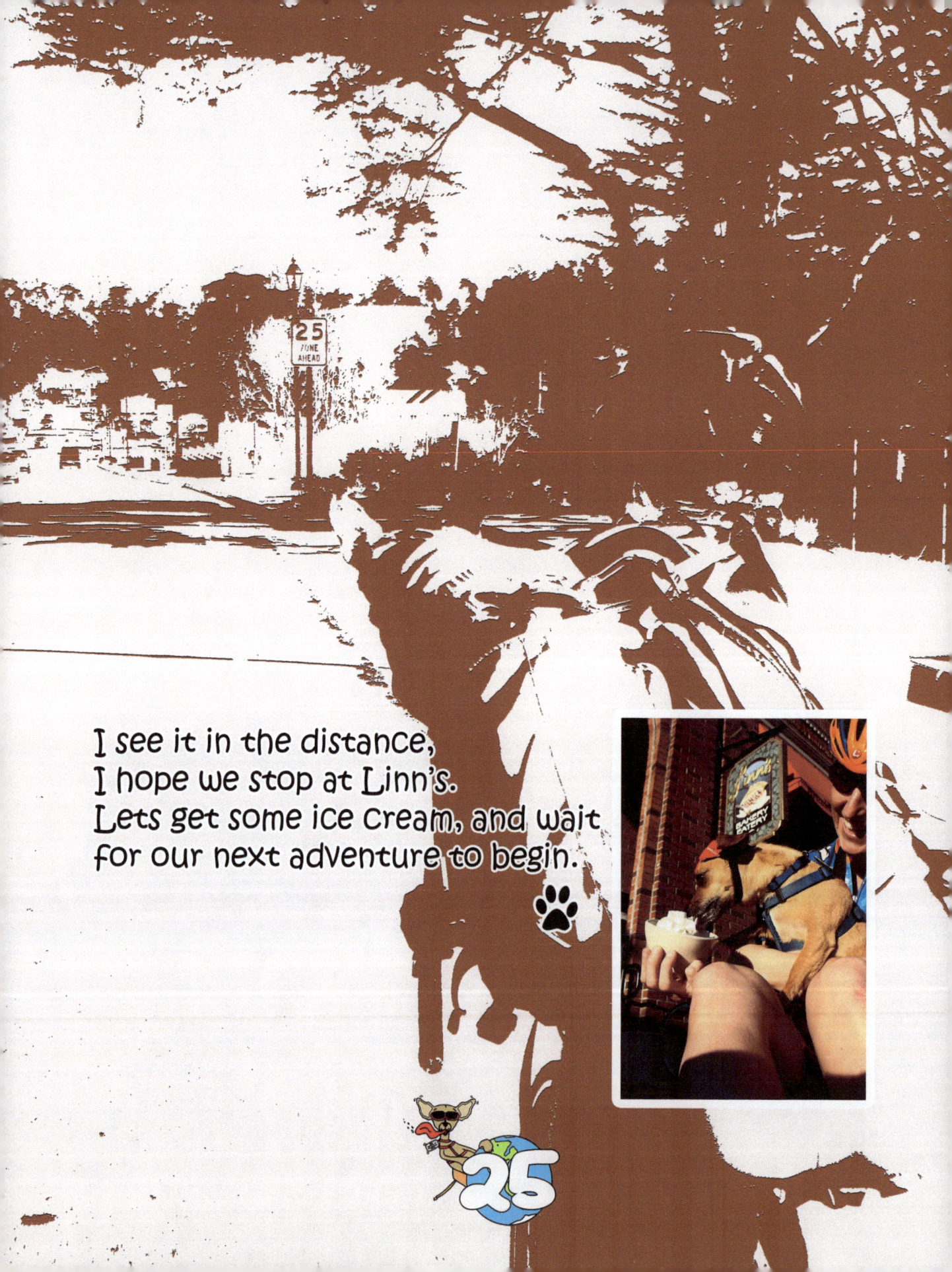

I see it in the distance,
I hope we stop at Linn's.
Lets get some ice cream, and wait
for our next adventure to begin.

Keep up to date on all of our new adventures at www.thegreatchiweenie.com. Check back often.

Adopt a pet. Ride a bike. Smile.

We wanted to show a few more pictures from our trip, so here is the challenge: Count all of the times that you can see me in this book, including the background shots and cover. Then go to www.thegreatchiweenie.com and click on the contest page. Anyone who guesses the correct number of GUS has a chance to win a prize (more details on the website). I'll help you on these few pages. HAVE FUN.

this is me #1

me #2

Me #3

Me #4

Me on cub's back #5

Me #6 and #7

#8
Me
#9

WWW.THEGREATCHIWEENIE.COM

www.ingramcontent.com/pod-product-compliance
Lightning Source LLC
Chambersburg PA
CBHW041221040426
42443CB00002B/43